AWAKEN
Steps and Stories to Guide You

Shellee Rae

Rae of Light Publishing
Ashland, Oregon

Awaken
Steps and Stories to Guide You

Dedicated to all the amazing women in my life, who express incredible strength and wisdom, infused with beautiful and generous hearts.

I'm deeply grateful for your presence, love, and reflection as I continue to evolve and expand.

I love you all.

Foreword

If you've been fortunate enough to read Shellee Rae's memoir, *Suffering ~ A Path of Awakening: Dissolving the Pain of Incest, Abuse, Addiction and Depression*, you know that she's lived through an extremely challenging life that has transformed her into a wise and compassionate human being. What she's survived is a suffering and darkness that I can't begin to imagine. Who she is now is an amazing healer and friend, one whose heart's wish is to assist others in healing and awakening into the divinely human beings that we are.

I first met Shellee Rae in 2007 in a "Waking Down in Mutuality" group in Ashland, Oregon. She was already by then a veteran of the spiritual path, one with a courageously open heart. Over the next year I watched her courage and determination tested as she passed through the fires of transformation, often in darkness and despair, becoming more and more fully her awakened human self, and ultimately coming to rest in the unlimited love and peace of the divinely human.

Shellee Rae's "awakening tips" come from that place of embodied wisdom and compassion that her life's journey has brought her into. Now she offers support and guidance to all who are ready to move beyond the known into a new life, a new world. As the poet Rumi says,

"The time has come to turn your heart into
a temple of fire,
Your essence is gold hidden in dust.
To reveal its splendor you need to burn
in the fire of love."

Blessings on your heart's journey with Shellee Rae.

Bob Valine, author, *The Second Birth*,
and *Dancing in the Fire*

Introduction

Awaken, like the companion book *Enlightenment*, shares with you some of the symptoms of awakening, and can support and guide you in your awakening process, no matter where you think you are in your seeming journey. Take your time reading through the chapters. Read one and hold it in your awareness for a day, or even a few days, practicing the ideas expressed. Give some space to feel into whatever might get stimulated in you as you read and as you carry the reading with you throughout the day.

Awakening, like becoming lucid in a dream, can suddenly change your relationship to everything. For many people it's a long, slow process. However, for some the shift can seem as extreme as instantaneously landing in the body with a thud, and waking up on a new planet.

The fire of transformation is wild and can be very disorienting (make sure you've checked the expiration date on your fire extinguisher)! You are the infinite, formless, nameless One, dancing in a world and in a form with limits. That's bound to create a rub and it's meant to! It's the spark, the impetus, the fire under our butts to awaken.

Awakening is rarely a gentle ride. If it were, there would be no stimulus to move. All that is unconscious, all that is lying dormant within, typically needs strong emotion or a crisis to shake itself awake. The mind creates these things when we are ready to move forward.

Burning in the fire of awakening can make you feel like you're going crazy. It's important to have a good support team, preferably a person or a group of people who are experienced in (and not afraid of) the stages of awakening. Who better to assist you as you pass through the proverbial eye of the needle?

Many traditions lead people out of the body to a transcendental awakening, which is only half of the truth of who you are. You are wholeness; perfect, powerful, and free. To realize that while acknowledging the limited humanness creates an opening that allows peace and happiness to lead you through life. You already possess everything it takes to wake up. Drop into the body and discover the missing piece of awakening.

Let's go together on this adventure. Allow me to assist you in discovering that the you you've been longing for has been here all along!

Success is not the result of spontaneous combustion. You must first set yourself on fire. ~ Fred Shero

No, Not This

Life has a way of occasionally bringing us things we'd prefer not to have. That's just the way it is.
It helps to remember that Resistance = Suffering.

Yes, preferences are perfectly fine (and so is suffering for that matter - it can be a catalyst for greater awareness). My preference and potentially yours too, is to get through the difficult times with as much grace and ease as possible. When we resist what's happening in life, internal pressure gets created by pushing against what's present, which contributes to and feeds the discomfort.

As I've heard said many times, pain is inevitable, suffering is optional. Personal experience confirms this is true.

I went through a 5-month depression in the late 90's when I got sober that I didn't think I would survive. I kept thinking 'if it lasts one more day I'm going to the doctor for pharmaceutical drugs.' My friend kept saying to me, "You've been anesthetized with drugs and alcohol your whole life, of course it's going to take some time to feel and heal all those emotions that didn't get felt!"

She encouraged me to curl up in the fetal position with the covers over my head and cry if that's what I felt like doing. It seemed crazy to me to give in to it. I kept thinking there must be something I could DO to fix it, or that there was something very wrong with my brain chemistry.

Her advice helped when I could follow it. A good cry, or just lying down and experiencing the void of life-force-energy, creativity, motivation, desire, or hope was the DOING that needed to be done. When I could allow myself to feel what "depression" felt like IN my body instead of following the many disastrous stories that I had about depression and what depression meant, it created movement in my system.

Even feeling what resistance to depression feels like in the body, rather than saying, 'no, not this!' can create an opening for movement.

Funny how soon we forget though...
I guess as a happy, healthy vegan with the title of "Healer", I thought I was smarter than the body. Five years later I went into another deeeeep depression that lasted for two and a half years. I went to every alternative healer, nutritional guide, energy-worker I could think of, spending thousands of dollars.

Walking home from a meeting one night I was complaining to a friend that I'd still not found the right magic to heal the depression and she whispered, "Have you considered just feeling it?" That was like a 2x4 upside the head.

I had great fear about feeling depression. I was afraid if I surrendered to it, dissolved into it, I might just end my life. I dipped into it gently off and on for days, allowing depression to be there, fully feeling with no

3

attempt to positive-affirm it away. The depression that had lingered for years dissolved very quickly. What a teacher it has been.

There's more to say about the above experience in reference to dark-night-of-the-soul and stripping away of self in order to access one's true nature. Perhaps I'll get into that later.

You may be asking what the heck this has to do with waking up, and the answer is everything. The missing key to awakening for me was being in my body, feeling how life moves in me - now, and now, and now...

Transcendence is the natural outcome of integration. Integration happens when we shine the light of awareness on our experience, share it with a trusted other when we can, and feel it, all the way in, in the body. I would guess the thud was audible when I landed. What a gift to be here.

"The body is shaped, disciplined, honored, and in time, trusted." ~ Martha Graham

OMG and WTF

This life journey can be so difficult at times. Our past traumas, conditionings, and the people around us can add to an already confusing situation. When in the midst of a whirlwind that seems to be stirring it all up for you, see if you can remember OMG and WTF...**O**nly **M**e **G**rowing, and **W**illingness, **T**ruth, and **F**eelings.

A **W**illingness to stay with the experience rather than anesthetizing it with the distraction-of-choice can create an opening for something new to arise. There is growth that is wanting to happen - that is why the experience was called in. What is your inner guidance, your gut, your heart, wanting you to become conscious of? Be willing to explore the deepest meaning of these difficult events.

As you explore and examine all the facets of the experience, it's important to tell the **T**ruth. How has life shown this to you in the past? Is this a place where you undermine your own inner knowing? Listen deep and know your truth then see if you can stay with it while sharing it, even in the midst of a whirlwind. Buddha says there are three things that cannot be hidden for long, the sun, the moon, and the truth. Your truth is there just waiting to be noticed.

As you surf the waves of difficulty, remember to drop into your body. Trying to figure things out in the mind is attempting to solve something at the same level that it was created. Feel what is happening deep in the body. What is the gut saying? Does tension arise when move into the thought-stream, away from your inner-guidance? Do you feel lightness when moving towards or away from the situation that has your attention? Feeeeel what your body is telling you. It is so wise!

Some of these growth opportunities can be quite humbling. It's not always easy to acknowledge what's been masked by beliefs or what's lurking in a blind spot. Consider honoring these bumps and bruises as part of your divine dance. We see when it's time to see and not a moment sooner.

When moving through the tangles of life, make sure to notice the Wisdom that arises as Transformation takes place, and the Freedom that is your natural state!

Smile and remember OMG and WTF.

"It's not hard to find the truth. What is hard is not to run away from it once you have found it." ~ Unknown

What Else is Possible

Life is knocking at the door of your heart. All you need do is open it.

The possibilities in life are infinite when we open up to the idea that there is more available to us than meets the eye.

Are you letting the past define your present moment? Is history repeating itself? Albert Einstein said, "Insanity is doing the same thing, over and over again, but expecting different results."

Rather than knowing or seeing from the old paradigm, it's possible to break the mold and create something completely new.

Take a look inside and ask yourself, "What else is possible?" See if you can live in the question. As soon as you know something, there is no room for anything new to be created. Living in the not knowing blows the doors of possibility wide open.

See if you can allow yourself to not know:

Who you are
What you are
Why you are here
The purpose of life

And while free-falling, feel all the edginess that comes with not-knowing. This is like throwing a wrench into the works. The old patterns begin to fall apart. The neural network will not be able to fire in the same old way and transformation takes place, birthing a beautiful new you.

Life is infinite. You are life. What if it's as simple as that? What if the conditioned ideas that you've bought into are the only things limiting you? What if you are an exquisite, priceless and unique gift that the world is just waiting for you to open? NO one can be a better you than YOU! Your particular you-ness is so needed in the world.

Thank you for shining your light so brightly.

"If one feels the need of something grand, something infinite, something that makes one feel aware of God, one need not go far to find it." ~ Vincent van Gogh

You Are a Gift

Shine, shine, shine
As bright as you can!
The time for holding back is past. Drop in and see
where you are clinging to old ways, old wounds.

Feel into the remnants of pain, fear. Give it a big,
loving hug, and kiss it goodbye. Life awaits you.
Freedom is here, now.

Can you see how lingering in the past is a trap?
Continuing to keep the past alive in the present
moment, and feeling dissatisfied with the way life is
showing up, is like going to the shoe-store and being
upset that they're not serving pizza. As far as I know,
shoe-stores will always serve shoes, never pizza.

If you are looking for something different, it's
important to go elsewhere. See if you can notice any
repetition, or a trance-like state that is operating just
below conscious awareness. That habit has you

reacting in the same old way to the same old thing. Sigh! Shoes again?

This is not to discount the great relief that comes from feeling whatever it is that is coming into your awareness. You may find yourself becoming sad or quite angry with something someone is saying or doing; see if you can allow yourself to feeeeel that. Stuffing it will only store it in your field to be dealt with later. Typically, the feeling that is arising in the moment is an opportunity to heal and integrate an old emotion or wound that was either completely swallowed or only partially digested.

The traumas, pain, suffering, and depression I've experienced in life are the gifts and great teachers of my present life. As Tagore so eloquently said, "When I stand before thee at the day's end, thou shalt see my scars and know that I had my wounds and also my healing."

Life brings us the most appropriate people and events

to shake loose the frozen places in us that are in need of feeling and healing. As we are freed from the pains of the past, our scars become signs of experience, wisdom, gifts of hope and healing that can be shared with those around us, often without even saying a word. Your field will reflect more light and that will have an effect on the people around you.

You are a gift to the world, touching and serving life in more ways than you will ever know. Mmhmm! Thank you for being here, now.

"Here bring your wounded hearts, here tell your anguish; Earth has no sorrow that Heaven cannot heal." ~ Thomas More

Fierce Heart

Are you ready for change? Will change mean letting go of something? What are you afraid of? Losing someone, or something? Not-knowing what the new life will look like? Change for most of us means letting go of what no longer serves our highest good...often the past.

Letting go of the past does not mean that you're in agreement with it, that you like it, or that it didn't happen. Allowing the past to stay in the past only means that you are no longer willing to let it taint your present experience.

Even something as "minor" as the argument you may have had this morning can create a feeling of heaviness later. It's important to feel all the feelings that get stirred up, and talk about it (when you can) until the charge is gone. This creates healing, integration, deepening, and there is less chance of it leaving residue to be triggered by something else later.

When I got sober in '97, I remember struggling with how to live a happy, productive, and free life when everywhere I turned, the life I was living was a mess! I didn't know that I was all tangled up in a web of blame, anger, shame, and pain. The mess of my past was just recycling and validating the mess of my present, confirming over and over again what an awful life I was trapped in. I used to cry out to God, "Please just take me now because life is not worth living!"

The quandary I was facing was that I was mentally, emotionally, physically, and sexually abused for many years as a young girl, and it was still affecting my self-esteem, self-worth, and relationships. However, if I moved on from the wreckage of my past, I wondered many things…

- What would it mean to move on?!
- Who's to take responsibility for my dysfunctional way of living?
- Will moving on, no longer crying "victim", mean I'm okay with what happened?
- Will it look like I'm giving it the ole thumbs-up?

- Will I have to take full responsibility for my life today?
- Does it mean I will no longer be able to use my past as the reason for my life being such a mess, (and it is such a mess, and it's not MY fault)!
- Who to blame?

Oh, the immense internal pressure I was feeling...

With curiosity, and desperation, something was able to leak into my consciousness (enough pressure and a fissure is bound to happen). I began challenging the way I was operating, first with baby steps and timidness, and then with a fierce heart, consciously not letting myself get away with anything. I began asking a lot of questions when the story of victim would arise...

- Whose voice is this?
- Is this belief keeping me trapped?
- Do I feel lightness or heaviness in my body right now?
- Does this serve me in a positive or negative way?

- How can I move forward with this wound from the past and am I willing to do so?
- What would life look like if I no longer told myself this story?
- What positive, nurturing thing can I do for myself right now to feed self-love?
- How can I allow my painful history to be the catalyst for strength and courage today, rather than an immobilizer?

It wasn't easy moving on from the blame game. I had deep sadness, and white-hot rage that needed to be felt. I must have cried an ocean of tears. I also hung a punching bag and at times bloodied my knuckles while feeling the anger I had swallowed for so many years. This combined with support from others who had risen like a phoenix from the ashes of their pasts, began my journey of healing, integration, and eventually living a balanced, and free life.

Bringing my attention to the present moment over and

over was a powerful way for me to move out of the story of my past. Being present with what I was doing in the moment, whether it was preparing a meal, or taking a walk, kept all the insidious little voices from luring me into my story of woe.

Eventually, the identification with my past dissolved. When the line to that anchor was cut loose, the freedom and excitement I began to feel about life was immeasurable.

Oh what a Mystery...

"You are always a valuable, worthwhile human being -- not because anybody says so, not because you're successful, not because you make a lot of money -- but because you decide to believe it and for no other reason." ~ Wayne Dyer

Derail That Train

Are you *doing* with your focus on a projected outcome? How would it be to just BE with the doing, fully and completely present in the moment? See if you can let go of the desired outcome and move with the inner impulse of Life that is guiding you in the moment. Notice when you jump into the future following some belief, dream, or fear.

You can examine and challenge beliefs. You may discover that they are not yours. The thoughts you are having are not your own. They are leftovers from many generations and they've been spoon-fed to you since the day you were born.

None of what you *believe* is an original thought, it all comes from the past. The good news is it's not hard-wired. Look at what causes you to freeze, judge, reject, react, etc. and ask if that belief serves you (or the world) in any way, if not, thank it and say goodbye to it.

Yes, neurons that fire together wire together, however you can begin dissolving neuro-nets by confusing the program. Throw a wrench into the works by doing something completely different when you notice a pattern...

- jumping jacks while counting backwards
- sing, even if it's as simple as Happy Birthday
- run splash cold water on your face
- dance

Every moment is simply the effect of the last moment. What are you creating right now? Our lives are the outcome of the thoughts we've bought into. Can you just notice the thoughts as they arise without following them? When you get on the thought-train, it can take you for a very long ride out of the present moment, which is the only thing that is real. It's also the only place you can know the truth of who you are.

Everything outside of this very moment is a projection

based on what we've collected from the past. It is possible to derail that train.

Do you have a thought or belief that causes fear? Did you know that the physiological response in the body is the same for excitement as it is for fear? So what if some fear is just misunderstood excitement? The only real difference is the expected outcome. When focusing in the moment and not in some projected future (the expected outcome), is it possible to redefine that aroused energy as excitement rather than fear?

I've found it's much easier to move forward with excitement as my fuel. I sense you will too.

Throw the switch, derail that train, you may be surprised with what you find.

Let life be with you, not against you. If you think "My life will be upside down" don't worry. How do you know down is not better than upside? ~ Shams Tabrizi

When God Whispers

Just a few of years ago, I went into off-and-on moments of money-panic as I was very quickly depleting my small savings to pay all the bills. The voices from well-meaning loved ones were saying things like, "Don't you think it's time to get a job?" and "Minimum wage somewhere is better than nothing."

However, the Voice within kept whispering, "Wait." I questioned that inner voice a number of times asking it how long I was supposed to wait, and how many things I was meant to sell before something shifted for me. I'd been *waiting* four years at that point.

Following fear, I finally went and interviewed for a job, more than qualified, and was offered my choice of four positions in the company. As I was going through the interview process, it felt as if a boulder had landed in my belly. My body contracted at the thought of working for this company (which sold many food items I would never consider eating or offering to someone else), and the inner voice was no longer a whisper but now a deep urging to wait.

I contacted the company, thanked them and turned down the offers. Yes, at times I can still move in a direction that is counter to what my inner guidance is offering, however, I can no longer do it unconsciously anymore.

The money-fear experience felt like Life deepening my level of trust; trust of that which comes *through me* and not *from me*. I sensed that it was very important to be still and listen to the inner guidance I was receiving.

Almost another whole year passed before things began to change. If I'd been working forty to fifty hours a week at a job, I probably would not have accomplished all the inner work that happened over those years. My trust in Divine Guidance would not have grown as it has (which expanded my ability to work with others), and discovering this deep groundedness in the certainty of life's natural flow may also have alluded me.

I've done a lot of inner work over the years; 2004 - 2010 were the most challenging, exciting and grace-filled of them all. I could not be more grateful that I continued to wait, as softly requested.

When God whispers, I know it's in my best interest to listen. The ego is the voice of conditioned mind, the past, fear. We learn how to listen to our deepest calling by bouncing back and forth between the two. The bruises that occur from following fear are not a punishment from life, they are pointers, guiding us Home.

Body awareness, heart guidance, and listening in are ways to discern between fear and Guidance. A simple way to develop your listening skills…
-    Sit still with a decision and bring awareness into the body by focusing on the heart, belly, or breath.

- Notice what happens in the body when you make a decision. It might sound like, "I'm going to accept this job offer."
- Do you feel contraction or heaviness in the body or do you feel a lightness or excitement?
- Change it and say, "I'm going to pass on this job offer." Again, notice what happens.

Our bodies are so wise ~ it's where the Divine guides us. The mind is conditioned and directs us from the past. The mind leading the way is like artificial intelligence taking over. The mind is meant to assist, not lead.

Practice dropping into the body, following your deepest knowing, it's where the Juice is.

"Our bodies communicate to us clearly and specifically, if we are willing to listen to them." ~ *Shakti Gawain*

Watermelon Awareness

You don't need to learn anything else to awaken, you are already awake. Unlearn what stands in the way of knowing that! Begin unraveling the tightly woven thought-webs that keep you seeking for You in another form. Yes, I know, but Matthew said, "seek, and ye shall find", and at the risk of sounding heretical, I say stop seeking and ye shall find. Seek within is what I sense he was saying, that's where someone else said we'd find the Kingdom of God. ;)

The very act of reaching outward to find That which is here keeps you from recognizing It. In Psalms it says, "Be still and know that I am God." So simple ~ and it works.

Be still, bring awareness into that amazing and beautiful body. Consciousness, Life, God, the Self is not somewhere else...notice what moves here in this form called you.

You are IT...or perhaps *it-ing* would be a better way of describing this movement. Life is fluid, constantly moving, changing, evolving, expanding, and experiencing through innumerable forms, all complete expressions of the whole.

There is no your life, or my life, there is only Life, *life-ing* here in these forms that seem so separate. You standing up and saying "my life", would be like one cell in the body doing the same. You are part of the whole, just as much as one cell is part of the whole body, while in and of itself, whole.

Dive in deeply to the depths of what you call "I". Feel into all the nooks and crannies of the emotional body. Dance with the edges, feel into the triggers, and go even deeper. The mind wants to figure it all out, and the gold is in the body.

Every time you feel all the way through something that gets stirred in your emotional body you are giving awareness to an old, stored, unfinished owie,

something that was repressed for whatever reason.
Allowing yourself to feel it now, heals and integrates
that original wound, and brings more of you online.
Cool, huh? Not always easy though.

A simple example of a frozen experience...
I know someone who to this day says he doesn't like
watermelon. I remember how he decided that. He
loved watermelon when we were young, watermelon
and kids can be very messy though. He was scolded
for making a mess one time too many and eventually
turned down watermelon when it was offered. I
remember feeling sad about that because I knew how
much he really liked it. Watermelon awareness may
not be standing in the way of him recognizing the
Truth of who he is, it is however an energy leak;
energy is being used to keep that one at bay.

What lingers in the bowels of your being?

Even with all the work many of us have done, there is

still much to resolve for most of us, keep going, don't ever stop, it's so worth it!

Aum
That is the whole.
This is the whole.
From wholeness emerges wholeness.
Wholeness coming from wholeness,
wholeness still remains. ~ Isa Upanishad

Chrysalis to Butterfly

We are constantly being born. Each and every thing that comes to us is sent as a gift from the divine, to help us awaken, to assist us in remembering our true nature.

These "gifts" could be compared to hormones, which cause a reaction in both our internal and external environments. Often these gifts do not feel "good", and may very well look messy. They might push us to the edge of who we think we are, and that's their purpose. Our seed design needs this 'outer provocation' to stimulate transformation, the flowering of a new you, or rebirth.

See if you can free yourself from the story of the situations that are present and just feel the feelings that these things evoke.

Do you think the acorn screamed as it cracked open and began to sprout? Did the caterpillar panic when the hormone was excreted that began the process of chrysalis to butterfly? These events are programmed in the cells of the seed and embryo, and like you, in your soul.

The birthing process can look horrible to someone who does not understand what is happening. The outcome is miraculous. We only need remember to breathe, follow our inner knowing, feel the feelings, ride the waves, and share deeply with another when we can (even though it may feel vulnerable). While experiencing the challenges of being human, remember the beauty and perfection of life and its amazing metamorphoses.

What if you were to ask yourself as you're being challenged with a difficult situation if this is the hormone that stimulates the growth of adult cells and the programmed death of the larval cells? See if you can just be with all the movement in your body, and not go into a story about it, which perpetuates suffering. Feeling what gets triggered is the way through the difficulty.

If I'd known this while I was growing up, perhaps I wouldn't have used drugs and alcohol for 27 years to numb the pain of the sexual and physical abuse that I endured for years as a young girl. But then, that wasn't part of my soul seed. Life had something else in store for me, and for that I am grateful.

All the Power and Presence there is constantly bathes us in its ecstatic and eternal embrace ~ move through the rough spots and tap into your exquisite nature. ♥

"Did the tomato seed stop to wonder why its life force was imprisoned in the molecules of a seed? Did it look forward to the time when the seed would die of old age and set its life force free? No, it realized instead that it was in the seed for a purpose, that through the seed it could work its way to full maturity, to full fruition. It

realized that within the seed its divine pattern was contained." ~ Ruby Nelson

A Divine Mosaic

Holy, holy, holy. Life is so holy. All of it. Every bit. When I awakened in August of 2008, one of the things I experienced was a life review. In the space of timelessness, the eternal now, I saw my whole life, in chronological order, flash before me. I was weeping; it was beyond beautiful. The whole thing was like a Divine Mosaic.

Every experience in my life, right up to that very moment, was divinely infused and an intricate part of the exquisite whole. In that eternal breath, I was freed from the story of me. All the pain, joy, abuse, love, failure, triumph, and judgment was perfect and absolutely necessary to land me in that pristinely flawless moment. I could see clearly that if one piece were plucked from the scene, the whole dance, truly life as we knew it, would be changed. That's how connected we are. Seriously. One move effects the whole.

Though much of the trauma in my life had healed at that point, it became evident to me that there was nothing to forgive. I saw that Life was moving on its own accord, naturally, and that my not being aware of the purpose of the horrible events in my past was part of the recipe for my evolution and eventual awakening.

This is not to condone abusive behavior, only to free oneself from the past, alleviate suffering, unhook from fear, and to bring awareness into the present moment. Resisting the past only gives it power. The war on drugs, cancer, etc. will never be won because what we resist persists; Jesus knew the truth of that.

Matthew 5:39 says...
But I say unto you, That ye resist not evil: but whosoever shall smite thee on thy right cheek, turn to him the other also.

In December 2012, a woman I know had an incredible experience (the short version): At 4am a total stranger (drunk) walked in off the street into the house where she was staying, and into her bedroom. She was awake with a terrible stomachache, headache, and had herbal caps lodged in her throat causing difficulty swallowing and breathing.

BOOM. The nausea, etc., switched off like a lightswitch in the face of potential crisis. He stood staring at her, then shut the door behind him.

Suddenly her Higher Self jumped into action and she became the hostess with the mostess. She welcomed him, showered him with friendliness and love, and led him to the kitchen for ice cream. She conversed with him about the nature of life and death, and the purpose of life.

After long dialogue she escorted him to the door, gave him a hug and sent him on his way. Just moments before she was having a panic-attack about the fear of dying, and in walked an intruder who, as it turns out, was having the same. Giving him the advice she needed to hear most not only diffused a dangerous situation but also helped him on his path.

Each person comes into our life through the grace of God offering us a gift ~ to heal, to break our hearts wide open, to remember the truth of who we are. When we can drop into the body and feel the feelings that get stirred with each encounter, rather than feeding the frenzy by listening to the story, or adding to the pain body (as Eckhart Tolle calls it), release happens naturally and the original wound dissolves. At this point, growth, expansion, and awakening can occur.

Look for the gift Life is offering you in the moment.
- Is this an opportunity to feel and heal?
- To speak a truth in the face of fear?
- To listen deeply to another?
- To remember the divine perfection of life?

Is forgiveness a viable path? Yes absolutely, until you get to a place of seeing that it's all holy, part of this sacred dance, and that there's nothing to forgive.

"Forgiveness is the fragrance that the violet sheds on the heel that has crushed it." ~ Mark Twain

Kundalini or the Brick Wall

Life has a way of clearing the path to God-realization in the most extraordinary ways!

Many of you are aware of the wild ride I've experienced to reach my current state, which is not static, by the way. The only thing that is not in flux is the Peace that holds it all. I continue to notice and release old beliefs, feel and heal childhood wounds, deepen and expand. Some years ago I had an exciting revelation - freedom isn't static either; there is freer than free.

When I woke up in 2008, I was struck with a great sense of freedom. My mind became very still (thoughts float by like silent clouds). I no longer identified with my past, and even though fear or sadness would occasionally creep in (and still does), there was no more suffering, only the feelings, and curiosity... *where is this in my body, what exactly am I feeling, how can I give this even more space?*

Over the next few years, I noticed that the freedom I was living had been muted by defining it - "I am free." I am freeing would be a more accurate statement. Isn't that exciting?! It just keeps expanding!

Some of the ways that life brings these awarenesses can be quite challenging (and life has many ways of shifting us). One of the most common ways of clearing the path to your God-self is through patterns and repetition.

When I got sober in 1997, one of the first exercises life blessed me with was developing healthy boundaries. No better way to get really good at it but to be inundated with people who have poor boundaries (like me at the time). It was like hitting a brick wall over and over, until I finally noticed what life was teaching me: how to say no in a way that it could be heard clearly, and received. Brick walls have a way of finally getting one's attention!

Another way of clearing the field is through kundalini

awakening. As I briefly mentioned in my first book, it is not something I'd recommend you do alone, if you have a choice. Mine were spontaneous awakenings. The first three kundalini awakenings were very painful, scary, and quite debilitating. I thought I might die. By the time I had the third one in March of 2011, I was in complete surrender to the fire ripping through me. Obviously I survived.

As I recovered from the blasts of liquid fire, the first thing I noticed was many buttons and triggers had been dissolved. I had a fourth kundalini experience January 1, 2013 and this time after the fire in my head calmed down, the energy was able to flow unimpeded up and down my spine and for the first time, it was quite pleasurable. The three previous big burns had cleared the path.

Kundalini or the brick wall? I didn't consciously choose either, they chose me. I'm grateful for all the ways that life frees me from that which no longer serves.

As you continue to evolve and clear from your field the debris that stands in the way of knowing that you are already awake, a conundrum for many people is how to rest and allow life to do what life does, and how/when to take action in response to inner guidance.

Presence is my answer. Shine the light of awareness on this very moment. There is no moment in the future or the past that is more alive with God than this one. See if you are making this moment the means to an end. If you are, notice that and bring awareness back to the present moment ~ make it the end. Period. Just now. And now. There is nothing more important than now.

"Man's freedom is never in being saved troubles, but it is the freedom to take trouble for his own good, to make the trouble an element in his joy... that in pain is symbolised the infinite possibility of perfection, the eternal unfolding of joy." ~ Rabindranath Tagore

The Story of M-E

"Who would you be without me?" screams the ego (or at least incessantly chatters).

This mind-entity (m-e) has many people convinced that figuring it all out will finally bring an end to the cyclical question of "why". However, "why" is ego-food. It's the hamster-wheel. It'll keep you churning and burning and even suffering because there is no answer to the question, not in a way that will satisfy the ego anyway. Figuring it out is the booby-prize. It's like finding the answer to an equation, useful for something but it's not the philosopher's stone. Um, so what if the square root of 81 is 9, are you at peace now?

Mulling it over and over will continue to feed the beast, giving it more fuel to twist and turn while it looks for a new angle or perhaps the thing that it missed the last time around...

The gold is in the body. God, Creator, Life is here, and oh what an exciting, mysterious, and magical discovery when you become aware of that (and so natural)! We have a body for a reason; be here in it.

The mind is a tool and not the master. Artificial intelligence has taken over and is running the show in so many people. True Intelligence comes in through the door of stillness within the body; it is gentle and points rather than making demands or pushing the big red fear button.

The m-e has many very important things to keep you busy in the thought realm. Notice when the m-e is throwing you bait. Some of its flashy lures are: you need, you should or shouldn't, you have to, you can't, why, you'll never, if only, what if, and on and on.

As you begin bringing awareness into the body, the m-e may go into great fear and get even louder - it sure did with me. It was keeping me in a loop pattern, just hovering above the open runway of the heart. The never-ending-narrator had a story, definition, criticism, and judgment about everything, and was shouting it loudly.

When I was able to feel the pain of what I was going through at the time, I would drop out of the story of m-e and into the body. It was amazing to occasionally feel bliss or peace simultaneously with the pain I was experiencing. This was when I discovered that my body had a direct connection with God, that Spirit was here in form and not in some voice just outside of me.

Life is moving perfectly, doing what Life does, expanding and contracting, inhaling and exhaling, laughing and weeping, birthing and dying. The pounding I took from the m-e was necessary to finally crack the cosmic egg. Noticing the m-e and its insidiousness while keeping awareness on my body eventually released me from the m-e. Once I was freed from the babbling beast, Creative Inspiration was able to flow through me; the Infinite Love-Force that guides and holds and directs me was now in the commander's seat and "I" rest easily as the co-pilot...whew, what an easier flight from this vantage point.

Keep it simple. When you can, notice the mind and its chatter, practice taking two conscious breaths while bringing awareness into that magnificent and beautiful body. Allow yourself a few moments of feeling deeply; 70 (or so) trillion cells are vibrating with God. Wow.

"There is but one temple in this Universe: The Body. We speak to God whenever we lay our hands upon it."
~ Thomas Carlyle

The Impetus to Evolve

What an amazing and miraculous vehicle for life to move through, yes you, wow! Every movement, every breath, every moment is perfect, mhm, oh yes!

I've had many people ask me, "But what about the problems in life?"

Check in and see how you respond to life when difficult situations arise. Do you relegate difficulties as less important than the joys in life? Is there some idea or story that it should be different, that pain is not as valuable as peace?

Feel into the challenge and shine the light of awareness. Difficulties are precious pearls, gifts for us to receive. They are a magnificent part of this self-correcting system called life, and they are the impetus to evolve.

Identification with story is the hamster wheel, creating

a loop that keeps you trapped in the thought realm, causing more tension, contraction, and confusion. A story about what is arising is the necessary ingredient for a "problem". A projection, conditioning, judgment, or labeling is what sustains it. Problems cannot survive in the present moment.

Check it out. See if you can notice resistance to the way life is presenting itself right now. Stop, take a breath, put awareness on your body and feel whatever you are feeling. Is there a problem without the story? Just here. Now.

You don't have to write a new story about it, nor deny that you are being challenged with something difficult or painful. Just notice when the mind makes up a story about it and don't take the bait.

Before I got sober and then discovered NOW is the only thing that is real (and everything else is a projection or the past), I had such a loud and constant-chattering committee in my head. It was comparing, criticizing, judging, blaming, and telling me how it's always been or always will be.

I thought for sure I'd eventually go mad with all the noise, or that my brain would soon (and hopefully) spontaneously combust. What happened was something closer to the latter. It finally just burned itself out. Everything got quiet. It did get louder before the pop though. However, I just kept tunneling into the body, no longer listening to the voices, instead looking for an emotion or a physical feeling to put awareness on.

See if you can move with the pressures of life as you would with an awkward dance partner. It's okay to feel clumsy and uncoordinated. That's actually a sign that something is shifting. Look for the sweet spot in the feeling of discomfort. It's possible to feel comfortable with uncomfortableness.

Resting with life as it is, we become aware of the Peace that holds it all.

"Sometimes you have to lose your mind before you come to your senses." ~ Peaceful Warrior

Down the Rabbit Hole

Are you feeling a bit like Alice tumbling down the rabbit hole, or like Dorothy and wondering where the heck Kansas went? If not, you must have an incredible sense of balance, deep grounding, or perhaps powerful denial.

The energy shifting that is going on right now has many people in a dizzy-tizzy at times ~ self included. Hold onto your hats because it's not over yet! As a matter of fact the energies will be accelerating throughout 2013.

During high energy times the veils get very thin and things may seem strange in your world. I've recently received spontaneous initiations from spirit and am now occasionally seeing dear ones who have passed over show up during sessions offering gifts and messages for my clients. Trippy.

The winds of great change are upon us. The planet and

our souls are calling in higher consciousness here, steadily increasing our vibration. Denser energy (old emotional and physical wounds, shadow, etc) cannot withstand this new frequency and are up for feeling, healing, and release. I sense that whatever is in the way of our greater work and joy is being swept clean from our fields.

I've spoken to many who have changed jobs, careers, had relationship shifts, and let go of certain practices when they could no longer fight the pull of change. I've heard it said that when the pain of not changing becomes greater than the pain of changing, we change. I've also noticed this process tends to move much more quickly these days.

What's the best way to get down a rabbit hole without injury, you ask? Free-fall ~ perhaps even grease yourself up and jump. I hear many are resisting the shifting or going into fear and running to doctors for a diagnosis or pills.

Some things I find helpful for me; barefeet on the earth, time in nature, grounding foods, exercise (just move your body), toning, fire breathing, primal screaming, and tuning into my inner world. I also visualize my light body expanding, it seems to give me more space to be here in a physical body.

A few signs of vibrational increase:

Vertigo
Restlessness, lack of focus
Sleep change ~ sleeping a lot or not much at all
Diet change
Seeing flashes of light ~ external and/or internal
Senses super heightened ~ smell, hearing, taste, touch
Mood swings
Can't track time
Heat bursts in body
Pressure in heart and/or palpitations
Love overflowing for all
Sudden shifts in preferences
High pitches/tones/knocking/pressure in your ears

Purging your space

Feeling overwhelmed for 'no reason'

Kriyas (blasts of energy pulsing through the body
causing it to convulse or shiver)

Clumsy/awkward

Feeling like you don't belong here

The physical body will catch up as the energy integrates. Be with your experience as best you can. Do things that nurture you; baths, walks, snuggles, venting, etc.

Under the Influence of God

Over the years, I've had many people ask me the very popular and unanswerable question, "What is God?"

Here I go with the best words I can find, in this moment, to share with you what God is.

- The Holy Vibration that animates all form and non-form
- The Still-Point experiencing Its infinite potential
- Prior to thought
- Checkmate (no matter where you move, you can't get out of God)
- Here ~ Now

God is not a belief; God is Experience(ing), and ever expanding. Ones personal experience of God truly is unutterable. There are no words that will fully express what God is. As soon as there is a thought forming of what God is, there is limitation. There is no way to express the magnitude and divine precision of God. We can only continue to point.

It is possible to experience your more expansive self, or God-nature. I know many of you have read my first book, Suffering ~ A Path of Awakening, and may know this blip; this seems like an appropriate place to retell it though.

Awareness has expanded so much at times that the local self seems like such a funny trick that I am playing on myself. An example: I went to Mount Shasta to pick up some class supplies and on my drive there, my awareness expanded. Gradually I became aware that I Am so Big. I am all of It and nothing is moving separately from the whole and it seemed so funny to have all my attention on this "little me" driving in this little vehicle, moving around in myself [formless] and not really going anywhere at all. I felt like I should have a sign displayed on my vehicle: "Caution, driver under the influence of God and may be in an altered state."

How to get there? Be still. Go within. God is not somewhere outside of you.

Attempting to think your way to God-awareness will not work (as my experience has shown me). Quieting the stormy mind is a good first step to experiencing beyond the seemingly limited human self.

Notice there is conversation and activity going on in the head, a critic picking things apart, dissecting, rearranging, arguing, etc. Observe the constant narrator commenting on everything, saying what it is or isn't, judging, analyzing, limiting, and on and on. Being aware that there is chatter in the head is the first step, and bringing your attention into the body is the next step.

Take a breath, acknowledge that you are thinking and then drop into the body. Find something, anything that you can focus on, physical or an emotion, and give it your awareness. Become breath, or sadness, or backache. Let it have all of you. Dissolve into your experience. Do it over and over as the thoughts intrude upon your body-awareness focus. Eventually the thinking mind will get quiet. It'll say, "Hey, the last 100,000 times we interrupted, s/he didn't listen so fuhgeddaboudit." That's the ego (or false-self) being right-sized.

This practice not only helps to heal old wounds, and move stagnant energy, but it will also train the mind to be still. The snarly tangle of thought-forms is the very thing that is in the way of experiencing the Peace that holds it all.

It seemed impossible in '97 when I began meditating that my mind would ever be still. I was so addicted to thinking that I would pause meditating over and over to think about something for a minute or to write it down so I wouldn't forget (it was sooo important!) and then go back to my meditation. My mind was devouring me like hungry piranhas.

Whenever I considered dropping into the heart and allowing thoughts to pass on by, my mind would scream, "What?! Who's going to finish thinking these important thoughts, if not me? The world will turn to chaos!" I had so much going on in my head that needed my attention that I couldn't imagine not continuing to think through all these very important thoughts, to the very end, until resolution, and all the loose ends were tied up, all t's crossed, i's dotted, and on, and on, ad infinauseam. There did not seem to be an end to the train.

Today my mind is like a still lake with silent thought-clouds passing overhead. The clouds do not create a ripple on the water, nor do they leave a trace on by the unrippled mind. What a precious gift.

"Be like the bird that, pausing in her flight awhile on boughs too slight, feels them give way beneath her, and yet sings, knowing that she hath wings." ~ Victor Hugo

The Dance of the Ego

Ever notice how clumsy, awkward, or foreign something feels in the early days when you're first learning how to do it? It doesn't matter what it is, typically there's a period of time that passes before one feels confident, skilled, and comfortable in their new ability.

I've worked with many people over the years, supporting them in the challenges of life - be it relationship, healing, shadow stuff, or awakening. A common experience that I hear from people as we work together is a feeling of awkwardness, unsettled, or weirdly-not-themselves. "I must be doing it wrong!", is the frequent fear. I always get excited when I hear of their self-consciousness because it's a sign that something is shifting.

When we learn a new way to respond as we break the old patterns of reaction, there is an adjustment period. The whole system can seem a bit wonky; the foundation of the ego is being chipped away and this can cause a feeling of off-balance. It's a new way of being. It's throwing a wrench into the works and synapses are no longer firing in the same ole way.

Showing up in a new way creates openings for those around us to do the same. At times it can be challenging as we undo the training that has been done with those close to us. They expect us to act in a certain way and when that behavior or character doesn't show up, it may be off-putting for the other. Just keep BEing. They'll adjust, and potentially grow.

While BEing, see if you can be with the feeling of awkward. If you trust the person you're with, talk about it. Name it and claim it!

"Hey, I feel like a total oddball right now, I'm not quite sure how to relate to anything that we're talking about and I have a tight feeling in my gut that if it had a voice it would say RUN...", etc. Once you get comfortable with feeling uncomfortable, you can expand the practice from your network of close family and friends to people you're not as familiar with.

It can be very healing to reveal the deepest truth in the midst of the experience. Just be a run-on sentence for a bit, continually putting words to what you're feeling as you dance with awkward. Imagine you're learning how to dance with two-left-feet, or walking on a trampoline with a tray full of beverages. Awkward, shaky. It can help lighten the experience by remembering to not take it so seriously. This practice allows for ego diminishment, or a softening of the ego's grip.

I was out kayaking with a friend on Saturday and could see he was getting a bit too much sun. I suggested he might want to cover his legs with the (lilac and baby blue) towel I'd loaned him. I noticed hesitation, then he pulled it out and covered up...clumsily. I could see him shifting it, scrunching it, and accidentally dragging parts of it in the water before he voiced, "I feel like an old lady with this thing on me." I smiled and said, "Mhmm, feel that."

The ego says 'what will people think?', and immediately wants to rebuild any diminishment that may have just happened.

It's so valuable to feel the squirm; let more of that false-self fall away so more of the splendor of your exquisite, infinite nature can shine through you.

Wahoo! as more of That comes through!

A Ch'an master contradicted himself (seemingly) a good twelve times in the space of an hour. Exasperated, a disciple laid bare the succession of contradictions before the amused and benevolent gaze of the master, whose entire response, simply said, without trying to justify himself in any way, was, "Really, how strange and marvelous! I'll never understand why the truth is always contradicting itself!" ~ Eternity Now by Francis Lucille

What's Here Without Reaching

Our purpose here is to live, to just let Life dance us in every moment. There is nothing beyond being here that we need to do. Yes, I know, it sounds crazy to state this so simply. However, Life does magically go before us and prepare the way. Life knows where she's going and it's easy to follow her lead when we are present.

You are the Awareness that is aware of every experience in Life. When attention is brought into the body, it's not to say that that's where "enlightenment" is, it's to soften the distraction of the seeking mind that says you are not awake (and many other crazy things), and that something else must be "IT".

Thoughts come and go, awareness (you) does not. What's still here when thoughts are not? Be still and know that you are God ~ incarnate. Holy smokes! Stop pretending that there is something more magnificent than magnificent you.

Let's consider the words, "human being", which is really a misnomer since most people are human-doings.

"Hu" means God. In Sanskrit "Man" means mind. And "Being" is the state of existing. *The mind of God being here in form.*

See if you can let that take the pressure off whatever you think you should be doing in your life. You can't get it wrong. This is God's game and when you recognize what's here without reaching, you are free. God BEing through people (and everything else), and as humans, we get to be conscious of It. Awesome.

Practice being here. Presence is the only thing needed to become aware of the magnificence of God in form. All the pain, bumps, zigzags, and difficulties in life are fertilizer for growth. Your expanded Self has called these things in to help shake you awake. They are typically experiences that will bring attention to the immediate moment, which is what is needed to recognize your Holy Self!

It's easy once you get the hang of resting in awareness...just waiting for Inner Guidance to direct you. We've been conditioned to jump into the mind and go into a whirlwind of thoughts to try and figure things out. I used to get headaches from working so hard in the thought realm, following every thought to the end, looking for a solution through all the things I thought I knew. It's possible to be free of that churning.

When making a decision now, I wait for an inner yes. If I don't get a "yes", it means life has something else in mind for me, so I wait. I wait for Life's Impulse to show me the way. It comes softly through me, not from me.

Answers from Spirit come from stillness. Guidance doesn't come from something that I figure out in my mind while listening to a barrage of thoughts from my past telling me what I should or shouldn't be doing.

Life, here, now, defines me, over and over again. When we shine the light of awareness into the body and listen, we can feel Life's guiding touch in every moment.

Living free is counterintuitive to what most of us are taught. There doesn't have to be struggle or suffering. One can wake up in the midst of the worst scenarios and be full of the Joy of Life.

"Forgive, O Lord, my little jokes on Thee And I'll forgive Thy great big one on me." ~ Robert Frost

That 4-Letter F-Word

Is your mind holding you hostage in the past? Creating over and over the same small, uncomfortable world that you're wanting to get out of?

Fear, worry, and anxiety are products of the mind, created from the past. Worry is buying into an idea that something is going to happen that shouldn't happen, or that something isn't going to happen that should. It's being attached to a particular outcome that the mind has created rather than resting with how Life is presenting itself ~ naturally. Attachment creates fear and fear can evolve into suffering due to the many stories the mind creates about possible outcomes of any particular event.

Worry is believing that you are separate from Life, and that you may be able to control the outcomes of this naturally occurring, organic experience, if only you try just a little harder.

All change occurs in the moment when the issue is recognized. Worry does not change anything but ones health. Not knowing what the situation truly is or what it's for, creates an opening for the Creative Impulse to move you. Uncertainty always resolves itself in the Now, as one continues to move forward.

Life knows just exactly what Life needs in every single moment of Life...always has, always will. Fear or worry is some thought that Life might get it wrong, which of course is not possible.

What if it's possible to be free of all those stories, and that crazy narrator who seems to prattle on and on about everything?

Some questions you might consider when the mind is throwing you bait:

- What are you afraid of?

- What is the worst thing that might happen if you let go and just allow life to present itself the way it's presenting itself?
- How "bad" would that worst thing be?
- Is it true or is this just a belief?
- Is there some fear that Life might not handle this one? That something might happen that is not meant to happen? That Life might make a mistake if you're not in control of things?
- Are the urges to control coming from a deep gentle feeling of guidance or is it coming from fear?
- When you think of taking control, do you feel a sense of lightness, or do you contract and feel a bit heavy?
- Are you saying "No" to any part of your experience (resisting)?
- What would it be like to let go of the reins, feel the burn of not being in control, stay with your experience without knowing what any of it is for, and wait for Love to guide you?

Situations come and go. People, animals, and

things come and go. Suffering happens when we try to hold on. All is well! The Universe is big enough ~ you are infinite enough ~ to create an opening for solutions to flow into existence; sometimes it doesn't look like we might imagine.

See if you can stay with your experience rather than following some story about it. If you're listening to fear, you won't be able to hear the voice of Wisdom.

What if freedom is just being here? Not arguing with what life is presenting in the moment. Saying yes to what it is that you (from a higher perspective) chose to experience in this moment. Not listening to, or creating another story about it. Just allowing whatever it is that is showing up to show up. Yes Life, even this. Yes, I say yes.

Does the flower have thoughts, judgments, or a story about how it's flowering or not flowering? No, it just flowers. Life is inherently designed to be this simple. Just flower. Follow the natural flow of Life's deep guidance. It is possible, plausible, and practical to be free. I'm hearing more and more people using that 4-letter f-word. Hallelujah! It sure makes my heart sing! You are designed to be f-r-e-e!

"Oh, the places you'll go! . .

KID, YOU'LL MOVE MOUNTAINS! . .

Today is your day!

Your mountain is waiting.

So...get on your way!" ~ Dr. Seuss

Are We There Yet

Imagine you are on a mystery trip travelling at 70 mph to an address when all of a sudden blinking signs warn you of road construction ahead. What do you do? Yes, you slowdown of course. Eventually you get through the slow spot and are moving at a good clip again.

The excitement builds as your speed increases, and the mind is wondering about the mystery destination. What will it be like? Why have I been sent there? Who else will be there? What will I do when I arrive?

Further up the road as you are coming into a city area, there is traffic congestion and again you slowdown, and again eventually you move through that sluggish area. All the while, whether road construction, heavy traffic, weather hazards, etc., you are still travelling.

During the times of adjustment to your speed for the road conditions you can fume about it, struggle and stress about it, or you can rest with what is arising in the moment. Ah-traffic. Oh-construction. Hmm-detour. You could even get curious about it and wonder what this pause in your path is for, or what it might be creating just out of your limited view, or simply enjoy the scenery and the ease of slow travel.

There are many times in our lives when we hit walls, when flow feels frozen, or we land in flatness, feel disconnected. These times are just as important (if not more so) as the times of joy, connection, flow, etc. They are times when the road is being repaired, the landslide is being cleared, a treacherous accident being avoided, and it's important to slow down from 70 mph to a speed that's more appropriate for the surroundings. You are still moving, it just might not look like you thought it would.

Finally, after the many miles, bumps, pauses, and detours, the GPS announces you have arrived at your destination. You are greeted in an empty lot by the One who sent you and you are questioned about all the details of your journey.

The One who sent you eagerly asks if you enjoyed the magnificent red woods along the Avenue of the Giants. Then with much enthusiasm points out the detour that took you along the jagged coast for amazing views there. Next you're asked how you felt as you crested the summit and glimpsed that stellar vista. And if you stopped at the sweet mom & pop cafe, or camped at the elk sanctuary, and on and on the questions come at you regarding the many areas you passed blindly through, while focused on some projected landing point.

Rather than saying, "Are we there yet?", consider the possibility that there is no there, only Here. The clearing of conditionings, concepts, and patterns (which prevent you from recognizing that the destination is wherever you are) will free you from the box of limited living.

Allow the slower pace, the flat times, emptiness to be there. No thing to struggle with or fix, it's clearing debris from your field so that you can see more clearly what's here, and move more freely in That.

When we open our eyes with our hearts open too, we can easily detect the miraculous in every moment. Nothing better or more miraculous than Now!

"The magical mystery tour is waiting to take you away, waiting to take you away..." ~ The Beatles

This Is All There Is

If you were aware that your time here in this life was about to end, how long would your list of incompletes be?

Are you holding onto something for the right moment to set it free; be it an acknowledgment, a vacation, a forgiveness, appreciation, love?

What if this is all there is?

We have no idea how long we'll be here in form, though many plan into the future as if it's a done-deal. Some people neglect their own heart's callings, and squirrel-away practically everything in hopes of having a big cushion at the end. Those folks miss the joy of living today by being focused on some perceived life in the future, which typically causes fear and anxiety as they try to make all the right decisions.

Simply stated, just do it. Do the very thing that you are

being deeply guided or called to do. Watch for the opening and then leap. Trust that life will catch you.

A friend often said to me (in early sobriety), "Life is to be enjoyed, not endured." I thought he was either crazy or on something because my life sure was painful, and challenging. I had a lot of ideas (programming) about how life on the outside should look in order to be happy and free. The externals didn't match ideas I had about what life should look like, and there was a whole lot of suffering going on.

When I began relaxing my grip on some imagined future, it was much easier to follow the natural impulse of Life, and I began to recognize the beauty of just being here. All the pressure I was feeling from the future life in my mind that I thought was real finally began to dissolve.

You are the Infinite expressing in that amazing body all the brilliance of life in form! See if you can open up even more and allow the awareness of that to direct your movement in this world. Where is your heart pulling you? Where are your yeses? Are you resisting the gentle ushering of Life?

It's been my experience that simple questions create openings and they don't need answers from the mind. Just ask them and wait for guidance, synchronicity, something creeping into your awareness (usually more than once), and see if you can trust what comes to you. If you don't follow the nudge, notice how it came and how you denied your inner knowing. When, "I knew it!" arrives, make note and perhaps the next time you're guided, it'll be easier to let go and be led.

The time is Now. There is no future. This is all there is, here, now. Each moment a gift, an exquisite blessing, an opportunity, divine, whole, brand-spanking-new.

Wow.

"The price of inaction is far greater than the cost of making a mistake." ~ Meister Eckhart

Look in the Mirror

Look in the mirror...

Make deep eye contact with yourself.

Bring awareness to your heart and say, "I'm sorry for all the times and all the ways I've denied you(r) love. I love you."

When I got sober in 1997, I began doing a 'mirror meditation'. I would sit in front of a mirror, eye-to-eye with myself, and say over and over, "I love you." My mind would scream other things, usually very obscene things, or simply, "I hate you!" Besides the internal rebuttal, I did some pretty crazy things, like hit the mirror (I cracked one), and spit at myself (I had some deep wounding). It didn't take very long though before something began to seep through the facade of self-hatred. There was something there in my eyes that looked and felt more like love than hate, and the warmth that was radiating out began melting the long-frozen icecap of my heart.

God is here, emanating through this precious form in the mirror. There is no better way to connect with the source of All That Is than to look deeply within yourself. Many complain about the elusive nature of God, though God is always here, *closer than breathing, and nearer than hands or feet*, as Alfred Tennyson stated.

I had a belief for many years that God was somewhere outside of me, and that "He" didn't like me and that's why I was being punished (well, I had been "bad" you know). When through meditation, initiations, and spontaneous expanded-awareness states I began to feel what I could only describe as God living and flowing through me. I realized that it wasn't possible for God to dislike me.

Acknowledging the monumental inadequacy of words as I attempt to point to the unpointable; God is an ever-expanding, infinitely-experiencing, embodied, and formless, neutrality. The whole of life and non-life is God-experiencing.

A word that points to this Holy Vibration is ecstatic, and each experience unique and exquisite. The ecstatic resides in the longing heart that aches to end suffering (which is also where the ecstatic resides). It's all allowed, and it's all part of this divine and magnificent dance called life.

As sobriety evolved, and the fog began to lift from my mind, I noticed that I hadn't consciously chosen anything that had happened in my life. It seemed preordained somehow, guided by some out-of-sight Force.

All the zigs and zags of my life have purpose. Even though at the time I had not yet fully realized that, there was a relaxation that happened deep inside which helped me to forgive myself and others for all the perceived wrongs that had been done.

You are perfect, I am perfect, and our imperfections are perfect. Just as the sculptor chisels and smoothes to create a work of art, the imperfections are intricate pieces to our development.

Recognizing the love that resides here in this body-temple was a big precursor for the continued awakening to the awareness of God in everything.

I'm sorry for all the times and all the ways I've denied your love. I love you.

"A psychiatrist tore a picture of the world from a magazine and cut it into tiny pieces. "Take these puzzle pieces," he said to a young boy, "and put the world back together."

In just a few moments the smiling child returned with the completed picture. "How did you do it so quickly?" the amazed doctor asked.

"Easy!" said the boy. "I noticed that there is a picture of a man on the other side. I just put the man together and the world came out all right." ~ Steve Goodier's "Life Support System"

It's All Grace

Where is Grace not? Who defines Grace?

Grace is the opportunity to be here in a body and experience Life and ALL its undulations. God does not give "unmerited favors", or merited ones for that matter.

The conditioned mind often says, "No, not the bad things, that's not grace!" I have seen, heard, and experienced over and over the grace of some of the most challenging life situations. My greatest growth has come from my deepest pain. Great awakenings can come from the deepest sleeps.

It all has its purpose, to shake us awake, open our hearts more fully, show us our deeper selves, and bring us home to center, where we no longer identify with the clatter of the outside world.

Come back to center and see if you can rest in that

Still Point. Notice when thoughts arrive pulling at you like an incessant child. Watch how you allow the distraction to take you on a wild ride where one thought, like a fractal, opens to the ever-expanding, infinite web of thoughts or story. Rarely does resolution ever happen there; just an entanglement of conditioned ideas, old programs, and stories running, feeding itself like some obsessive, hungry creature.

Be alert and see if you can notice in the moment (or soon thereafter) that a thought has arrived. That's the place of choice. You can use single-pointed focus on a mantra, the breath, a feeling in the body, or you can follow the rampant barrage of thoughts.

Great things happen in silence. Have you ever noticed that the most creative solutions and ideas come while the mind is at rest, perhaps in nature, meditation, or even exercise? When the mind is peaceful, we're able to detect a more gentle Guidance, the voice of Love which cannot be tainted by fear. This is how wonder gets ignited, sitting in the silence of the inner world, not knowing what anything is for, watching, and waiting like a curious child.

It's all Grace, even the most seemingly dastardly things in life.

In the Nag Hammadi Library, "The Thunder, Perfect Mind" says,
"For I am the first and the last.
I am the honored one and the scorned one.
I am the whore and the holy one.
I am the wife and the virgin.
I am and the daughter.
I am the members of my mother.
I am the barren one
and many are her sons.
I am she whose wedding is great,
and I have not taken a husband..."

Grace is the brave soul who comes here to be despised so that I (as God-experiencing) may experientially know victimhood and the despicable. So that I may struggle with it (because of limited human perspective) and in my particular case, come to the other side of it. All of the personal challenges for the deepening of compassionate, greater loving, higher intuition, and now able to support others in their difficulties.

Be with the pain you experience, be with the joy you experience, be with the challenges and victories...just experience it all. That's why you came.

See if you can experience without labeling it while you wait for the mind to witness the miracle.

"3 And not only so, but we glory in tribulations also: knowing that tribulation worketh patience;
4 And patience, experience; and experience, hope..." ~
Romans 5:3-4 KJV

There's No Place Like Home

Are you living in someone else's reality? Seemingly controlled by rules, beliefs, and ideas? Trapped in an invisible prison?

Our limiting beliefs are like the invisible cell the hypnotist creates. The audience can clearly see that there are no confining walls, even though the hypnotized one is anxiously trying to get out.

Our conditioned ideas are the walls that are limiting us. They show us how impossible it is to get out but they're not real, they're imagined. What can make it even more concrete is that most of the people around us are under the same spell, and they're seeing the walls too.

Unlike the audience who can clearly see there are no walls while watching the hypnotist's mysterious show on stage, many of our family and friends struggle with the same invisible prison. All that is needed is for the hypnotist to snap their fingers and the walls will disappear.

Here's an opportunity to snap your fingers and snap out of it - question everything! Yes, everything. A 12-step friend used to say that to me in my early days of sobriety. I said to her, "Question everything?! What the hell does that mean?" She said, "Very good grasshopper, you've got it," and walked away.

As limiting thoughts come in, ask yourself if it's true. Pick it to pieces by asking things like, "Who made up that rule? What else is possible? Do I really believe that? Am I giving up my freedom to create what I want by believing this?"

Just because it's always been that way, doesn't mean it can't change. Until you take full responsibility for your life, you'll never know real freedom. Check your choices. What are you believing that's keeping you trapped? Keep questioning it until you get to the root, then you can pull the weed from your magnificent garden.

Awareness is key. Be intensely aware! Acutely aware! There is no better book, movie, or drama than your life - be there fully! Challenge whatever you think is "real".

You are amazing, magical, holy, and infinite. Abandon limitation, and return home to limitless joy, peace, and stillness.

There's no place like home. There's no place like home. There's no place like home.

"Argue for your limitations, and sure enough, they're yours." ~ Richard Bach

Love to Love

Mahatma Gandhi said, "Where there is love there is life." So simple a statement one can miss the true depth of it. And where there is life there is love, which is what oftentimes gets missed. Love is what's here. It's our natural state. It is what's at the core of all life.

In Taoism, wu-wei is an important concept. It literally translates as no doing or no trying, which is not the same as no action. Taoist tradition says that those who are in harmony with life behave in an unforced and natural way. A person in wu-wei spontaneously and effectively responds to life - effortlessly. Movement and action comes from a much deeper place than the mind, and is as natural as the body surrendering to the seductive rhythm of a song.

When we stop trying to think our way into something else, it's easy to see that love leads the way, then we can effortlessly follow where the Impulse of Life is taking us.

Plants, animals, and humans grow without trying. Planets rotate around the sun without "doing it". Ease of living is what happens when the ego is no longer in charge.

Relax into the natural nature of be-ing; stop trying to be something you are not. Notice if you are following the past, someone else's ideas or beliefs, shoulds of the conditioned world, and check in to see if they are counter to your beingness.

What is love wanting you to know more deeply about yourself? How does love want to express through you right now? Life is bringing situations, people, and events into your field for your greater good. Love at the beginning and end of all things is guiding you. Truly.

What would it be like to mark one day of the week as Love Day? A practice that might happen on Love Day:

Bring awareness into your heart for that entire day (or

as much as you can), and ask what you can do for love. Do this with all your decisions, appointments, errands, meetings, people, and movements. What would it look like to consciously bring love into all that you do? What would it take to keep the heart open, shining love on everything for just one day out of seven?

Ask not what love can do for you, ask what you can do for love. Then follow that.

Give up all notions of what love is and what love isn't and just love to love. Recognizing the love that animates all life and moving from that as your truest center quickens one's awakening, enlivens the spirit, diminishes the ego, unleashes joy, and blesses the world.

"Love is always bestowed as a gift - freely, willingly and without expectation. We don't love to be loved; we love to love." ~ Leo Buscaglia

Love to love - that in and of itself is the gift, for the giver and the receiver.

"Your task is not to seek for love,
but merely to seek and find all the barriers within
yourself that you have built against it." ~ Rumi

When Life Gives You Lemons

"Make lemonade" might be considered spiritual bypassing. I say pucker up baby. Life is giving you a great opportunity to know, and heal yourself on a much deeper level.

Where are those tight spots, rigid beliefs, attachments? What are you afraid of? How has the conditioned world clipped those magnificent angel wings of yours?

When I'm experiencing challenges, or not clear about what's being expressed, I remember to first breathe deeply, and then to internally ask myself questions like:

What am I feeling?
What am I not seeing?
How am I limiting flow?
What am I most afraid of here?
What is life showing me about me?

Questioning is like bringing a flashlight into a dark room. As we move the light around, things in the room become illuminated. By bringing the light of questioning into the space, and then waiting to see what's illuminated, we get a glimpse of what's hiding in the dark.

It takes courage, vulnerability, and trust to completely let go of needing a certain outcome when tangled in a dark, cluttered corner.

It can be messy unwinding from the grips of beliefs, and fear, and that's okay. Stay with it until the last little foothold softens. It can be humbling, and that's a beautiful thing. It's a way of quietly chipping at the foundation of ego. Recognize when the mind kicks in with a story or witnesses to build a case, and immediately drop back into the body. Stay with the feelings. This will thwart ego replenishment.

Seeing hardened ideas, feeling deeply into old wounds, and giving space for that energy to move is a great gift to yourself (and others).

As we continue to expand, and awaken, there's no room for dusty old clutter. It's of a denser vibration and the new lighter you can no longer carry it. That's the good and bad news. What's no longer supporting your awakening will be in your face shouting for release. You don't need to know what the 'original offense' was that created the trigger. This moment's trigger is the opportunity to release it. Feeling is healing. To see it is to free it.

When life gives you lemons, pucker up, make lemonade, and celebrate this grand opportunity.

"Surrender is not something that you can do. If you do it, it is not surrender, because the doer is there. Surrender is a great understanding that, "I am not." Surrender is an insight that the ego exists not, that, "I am not separate." Surrender is not an act but an understanding." ~ Osho

A Deeper Surrender

Surrender? How? Why? Who will be in charge!?
These were some of the questions that came up for me
when well-meaning people would say it to me.

It took many years of life surrendering me (which is
what eventually happens as we attempt to control life)
before I was able to let go of the reins and allow life to
have its way with me.

Surrender allows the most perfect, and situation-
appropriate sharing to come through. When
surrendered, the wisdom that is now able to flow can
be received and enjoyed by all who are listening,
including the one delivering it.

I can't tell you how many times people have quoted me
or reminded me of something I said to them and I
usually say something like, "Wow, really, I said that?"

Rather than rearranging old thoughts, beliefs, and

conditioned ideas of the past, then serving it again, life gets to meet each moment fresh and move unencumbered by the leftovers.

I gave my first book-signing in 2009 where 17 people attended. It might have been the first time in my life that I experienced what I would have defined then as complete surrender.

I walked up to the podium, quite nervous, not having any ideas about how to do it (had never even attended a book-signing), and when I read the first paragraph in my book, I silently realized, "This isn't mine. The book came through me, the book signing came to me, and none of this is mine." Prior to that I had always arrived prepared for events with manuals, handouts, outlines, etc., and with a projected outcome. This event was organic and had a life of its own. The flow was incredible, the questions were marvelous, the answers were magical, and the feedback was surprising.

Afterwards, people came up to me and said they felt I had listened deeply to their questions, and that they enjoyed when I paused while waiting for the answers to arise rather than just answering from a practiced knowing or preaching to them.

This is life serving life. When we get out of the way, magic happens. Prior to the book-signing, I didn't know that I could arrive not knowing how to do something, and be totally carried, have it just be done through me.

Since then I've discovered that miracles and magic happen all the time as I rest in a deeper surrender. Truly no-thing to do. Complete non-identification with what's coming through allows me to stay in a state of deep rest and not-knowing, while life itself effortlessly responds to every person and situation I'm presented with. The gift in this is that I get to experience and enjoy what's coming through too!

"The essential surrender happens within you; it has nothing to do with anybody outside you. The basic surrender is a relaxation, a trust - so don't be misguided by the word. Linguistically, surrender means to surrender to somebody, but religiously, surrender simply means trust, relaxing. It is an attitude rather than an act: you live through trust." ~ Osho

Crazy Stages of Awakening

In 2008, I was out walking when suddenly, in a whoosh, I was moving in (or as) fluid and entered into total stillness. I slowed my walking and breathing in this exquisite state that seemed so surreal. The sound was like being underwater breathing with an oxygen tank, except that I could hear my heart beating too. Nothing else around me had sound or relative substance to the dimension I was in.

I continued to float down the hill where I encountered three deer, a mother and her young ones. As we all stopped and our eyes met, instantly my heart became an inferno. Tears streamed down my face and I felt completely consumed by love. Like a deer in the headlights, I was frozen in place with these amazing creatures, experiencing infinite love for what felt like eternity, although was probably only minutes.

As the state slowly faded (leaving remnants of bliss), I flashed to a time with my older brother many years prior. I was sharing a story with him about seeing a couple of deer on a trail while I was out jogging. He smiled an enigmatic smile and said, "If you could sit in their hearts you would know something." I've always wondered if the schizophrenia he was diagnosed with was not illness but misunderstood sensitivity, and just part of the "crazy" stages of awakening. Most modern societies sedate and medicate people if they show signs of *insanity*. However, many tribes recognize those same signs as the stages of awakening and take care of their people while they are birthed into a new way of being here.

My brother's wise words struck me then and even more so in this more recent encounter. That's how it felt - like I was in the hearts of those deer, although I'm not sure if I was sitting in their hearts or if they were sitting in mine - we were all in the one heart I suppose.

Like Prasad, this exalted state was such a sweet gift from Source. It gave me just enough a taste of the

Divine to keep me from leaping off of a cliff; most of the time I was in such a burn that I didn't know whether or not I'd survive. Unaware of what was going on, I was deep in the throes of awakening and felt like I was losing my mind. Little did I know then that losing my mind was exactly what was needed.

Even with all the years of work I'd done (12-step, shadow-work, therapy, energy-work, etc.), I was identified with much, still programmed deeply, and quietly befuddled by life and my purpose here. I just wanted to be free.

The burn felt intolerable. I'd be out jogging and everything inside of me was screaming, "STOP!" I had a sense of wanting to shimmy my body just beneath the grass and lie there silently in the soil while finishing the gestation period, or decompose and be done with it all.

I was in a spiritual community that met weekly and there were nights I'd be holding onto my seat and rocking in my chair, feeling like I was going to spontaneously combust while waiting for a moment to speak. Eruptions of anger, sadness, messiness in relating, and inability to motivate myself to "do" anything, especially the daily practices (yoga, meditation...), were the norm for me during this period.

That which no longer served the whole was being reduced, and it was painful. When the fire gets hot enough, those things that do not support our truest essence will burn off. I popped. I survived. You will too. Don't go it alone.

I'm witnessing a lot of people waking up; what a gift to Mother Earth and to all of us here.

Be with what's showing up, breathe, scream, cry, laugh, go crazy, and re-Member.

You're in the arms of the Divine...ALL ways.

"All of our reasoning ends in surrender to feeling." ~ Blaise Pascal

The Tightrope

Are you hiding from your own Knowing?

You know that tug in the heart or the gut feeling you sometimes get when pondering something, the gentle undertone of some knowingness that is present?

That is innate wisdom guiding you, your higher self. What often happens though after we've been so wisely guided is the ego very quickly steps in, dredges up the past while analyzing what you've been guided to do (or not do), which invites doubt that then causes confusion, fogginess, or fear, and undermines the clarity you had just a moment ago.

See if you can recognize when this happens and say yes to your inner guidance.

Let go...

Let go...

Let go...

Life knows what it's doing...let IT do it, and you rest!

When we listen deeply, it's easy to tell the difference between ego and Guidance. Ego screams or demands and there is almost always fear or an emergency sense to its suggestions. Guidance is more like an offering. It gently points, and while resting with that, creative inspiration and ideas can arise that feel 'right' to move on.

When we listen to ego, things can get really messy very quickly (which can be a great way of teaching one to listen). When we listen to Guidance, there's a sense of perfect unfoldment...a flow, no efforting.

The more we follow the gentle tug of our inner knowingness, the stronger our confidence in following that knowingness gets, and the more we're able to trust when Life is showing us our next move.

It's only F.E.A.R; **f**alse **e**vidence **a**ppearing **r**eal. Because many of us have been trained to fear the unknown, often there is a lack of trust that we're doing the 'right' thing by just allowing Life to guide us.

Guidance is alive within - we only need heed it. Don't take the bait when the mind lures you with a potentially juicy story. The ego is just a frightened little creature that is very skilled at calling in many things from the past to keep us from moving forward.

I recall hearing this story of Charles Blondin who was the first person to cross a tightrope stretched 11,000 feet across the mighty Niagara Falls. He walked across, 160 feet above the falls, several times... each time with a different daring feat - once in a sack, on stilts, on a bicycle...

The crowd oooh'd and ahhh'd as Blondin carefully walked across - one dangerous step after another - pushing a wheelbarrow holding a sack of potatoes.

Suddenly he stopped and asked the audience,

"Do you think I can carry a person across in this wheelbarrow?"

The crowd enthusiastically yelled, "Yes! You are the greatest tightrope walker in the world. We think you can!"

"Yes, but do you believe I can?" Blondin continued.

"Yes, absolutely! We believe you can!" the crowd answered.

"Yes, but do you truly have faith that I can?" Blondin countered.

"Yes, yes! We have faith, we do!" they all cheered.

"Okay," said Blondin, "Get in!"

No one got in. The crowd said they had faith but their actions proved otherwise.

Say YES Life, even this. Nothing to fight. Nothing to screw up. It's not possible. It's just the ego gasping for breath and panting out words reminding you to play it safe! It's okay, you're held, you're whole, you're safe.

Faith is in the wheelbarrow, and it can carry you across the tightrope of life one breath, one moment, at a time.

Life is holding you and if you fall, it's only because there's something shiny there for you to pick up and share later.

"Tomorrow and plans for tomorrow can have no significance at all unless you are in full contact with the reality of the present, since it is in the present and only in the present that you live. There is no other reality than present reality, so that, even if one were to live for endless ages, to live for the future would be to miss the point everlastingly." ~ Alan Watts

Happiness Is

Did you know that your life is a prayer, that you are constantly praying to the Creator with your words and thoughts?

You don't need to be on bended knee, hands clasped, and eyes closed or looking upward. You are so loved, so free to create, and so powerful that the Universe responds to you whether you are in formal prayer or not.

We are the creators of our reality. Yes, I know, that can be a hard pill to swallow for some people.

I had no idea when I was going through the great challenges of my past that I was calling these very things in to develop myself, and nothing else could have advanced me more profoundly. The great level of unconsciousness I was living at tossed me about like a small craft in high seas. Finally I capsized, and just before drowning, miraculously found some footing.

I then began to make changes in my life by exploring what I thought I wanted. It began with a wish-list like a kid to Santa Claus, mostly with the word "more" in front of the item(s), which was actually focusing my energy on lack rather than the abundance I was requesting. Slowly that evolved to, "I want to be happy," and, "I want to wake up."

What I didn't yet know was that happiness is never caused by anything. It took some time to discover that true happiness is causeless.

If something on the outside (relationship, job, etc.) "makes you happy", that's the fulfillment of desire, not happiness. If happiness relies on an outside source, if it can be taken away, or if it can trigger fear of loss, that is not true happiness.

Happiness is not dependent upon something on the outside. It is a dropping of everything, of all the ideas of what we've been programmed to believe that will make us happy. Dropping illusions, ideas, and grasping will create an opening to discover the happiness that is our true nature. Happiness is a still point within you that desires No Thing.

What is your prayer? Do you know what you want? If you don't know what you want, how do you know that you don't already have it?

What are you reading, watching on TV, talking about, thinking about, worrying about, focusing on? Where attention goes, energy flows, and where energy flows, life grows. Bringing awareness and heart (gratitude) to the things you would enjoy experiencing has an energy to it that spins the universe into action.

Take full responsibility for all of it. Projecting and blaming others perpetuates the illusory dance of separation. Responsibility equals freedom. Come to the other side of the facade of all your beliefs, and reactions.

Just stop. All conditioning, and practices aside, what is

the untaught way to recognize yourSelf?

The Holiest of the Holies is right where you are. You are the One you are looking for.

"Know from whence you came. If you know whence you came, there are absolutely no limitations to where you can go." ~ *James Arthur Baldwin*

The Great and Fearful Teacher

June of 1997 I woke up in a hospital and didn't know how I got there or why I was there. I'd been there for 4 days and didn't remember anything. People came to visit, I carried on conversations with them and had no memory of any of it.

As it turns out, I had attempted suicide in an alcohol blackout.

Depression had always lingered in my field. I ran from it most of my life with drugs and alcohol. Back in the day, I wouldn't have identified it as depression; my mind kept telling me it was just lingering pain from the dreadful childhood I'd survived.

To make a very long story short, I got sober, did a lot of trauma-release work, eventually the depression was not so horrific, and I began to find new ways of dealing with it... until January of 2005.

I got knocked on my ass with a level of depression I'd never experienced before, and now sober, I had no way of running from it. This depression went on relentlessly until March of 2007.

In the midst of it, I thought for sure it would kill me; looking back, depression was my greatest teacher. The stranglehold it had on me was killing the remaining vestiges of hope I had that I might find something on the outside to fix my insides.

It was the beginning of the end of who I thought I was, what it was that made me happy, what my life purpose was, the meaning of life, etc...

I kept searching for something to fix me, heal me, or find what was "wrong" with me (and the world), while never allowing myself to deeply feel the great despair of losing all hope. Nor to completely feel what it was like to have no thing to prop me up, no solution to the seeming problems of the world or my life. It continued to wear me down, grinding off all the edges of who I thought I was, or what I thought I could withstand.

Then one night a friend said to me, "Have you considered just allowing yourself to feel depressed? Or if you can, even thanking the depression for its presence in your life?" It wasn't long after that when I discovered there is great strength through vulnerability, through surrender. I decided to let it have me, completely dropping into depression without a need to make it any different, without a lifeline, or a backup plan. Incredibly, the depression left. I suppose it was done with me, perhaps it had completed its mission. There was a sense of death on the other side of it. Something had died, a something that was no longer serving me.

A few things I discovered from the great and fearful teacher depression...

Personal drama can only happen when we identify with thoughts. Drama, story, projection, it all falls away when we are just here. Even the nagging question of 'what to do'...what to DO as we are BEING? Speaking, action, response, it all happens, guided by an unseen Force that knows no conditions, and that comes through naturally when one is resting, allowing all to be as it is.

All the questions of purpose, what to do, etc. come from the mind, which is not who you are. The mind can't threaten the True Self, it only threatens the idea of who you think you are. The mind's purpose is to wear you down and bring you back to the Still Point of Truth, which is not a voice rattling around in the head. It's the quiet essence that comes through you and guides when the mind has ceased its chatter.

Freedom from the hypnosis of the conditioned mind is a freedom that can't be taught or learned. Experiencing the joy of life through the sweet stillness of presence is a most natural and peaceful experience, no matter what is going on with the outside world.

Come and taste. It's something that can't be explained.

Just touch it, if only for a moment, let go of the longing that keeps you out of the most natural state, and just be here.

Come back to the place that the mind imagines it's lost. Drop every concern, struggle, woe, and see what's always here.

People who have not yet discovered their free essence may say you're mad because you no longer follow the conditioned mind. One person's idea of madness is another person's awakening. Once you know what's here, the misperceptions of others won't bother you anymore.

"How do you know I'm mad?" asked Alice. "You must be," said the Cat, "or you wouldn't have come here." ~ Alice in Wonderland

Choice is an Anchor

I've heard so many people ask about free-will, question whether we have choices here, and insist that they've grown, changed somehow through the many choices they've made.

While I'm sure more comfortable ways of playing the game of life are discovered everyday by using the plethora of methods of self-inquiry, shadow-work, energy-clearing modalities, etc., one must be careful to not get drawn into a game of chase.

Once I heal my childhood wounds, relationship issues, money struggles, obsessive tendencies, secrets of the past, then for sure I'll be pure enough to awaken.

I've been caught in that game of chase. It's a never-ending story. All the things I did or thought I ought to do to become clear enough, worthy enough, spiritual enough to awaken became one disappointment after another as I was left standing over and over again with my unstamped "Enlightened" card. Even though the techniques were helpful in various ways, the only technique needed to *be here* is to *stop looking* elsewhere.

Use as many methods, teachers, or gurus as you feel drawn to use. Getting your balance is okay, it's all okay. Recognize when you're getting attached to some method, or teacher, and then be sure to attach to one who is free, they will be your reminder to not attach to anything!

Just notice that you are relying on training wheels, and you won't know what a wild ride you might be capable of until you take them off. Once balance is achieved, then you can ride anywhere with anyone ~ just for the joy of it.

Until the idea that anything has to happen to be here -- complete, whole, fully alive, and awake-- is dropped, the illusion of separation and suffering will continue. Free-will, choice, these are ideas of separation.

The idea of choice is an anchor. Life knows where it's going, let It lead you.

When all choice is surrendered, then the Essence of Life itself moves freely through you, guides you, and carries you effortlessly through the dream of self. Then one is responding as a conduit of Life, rather than reacting as a separate entity attempting to conquer all the challenges of humanity.

Free-will, choice, these are just more clouds in the thought-storm. Be willing to let it all go, the idea of control, the joy, sorrow, suffering, the story, and then die over and over again to what's being born in each moment.

Here, just here, there is undefinable magic.

"Only words and conventions can isolate us from the entirely undefinable something which is everything." ~ *Allan Watts*

Dropping Illusion

Who is the self that is looking for the self?

Find the one who is looking and then you will see the silliness of it all. It's a cat chasing its own tail.

You are already here. When awakening happens, it's not because the self has been found, it is because the seeker has dissolved in the light of conscious awareness.

Eventually the mind-made self is seen and the game of chase ends as the seeker dissolves.

The unlearnable truth of you is not the cultivated self. The conditioned, programmed, running-on-autopilot self is not your effortless, natural, present self. This is the man-made or mind-made self, the illusory self.

Watch as the mind delivers more ideas of what to do to find the self. How many ways are there to find the self? Countless, I'm sure. The mind is very good at keeping one quite busy seeking through many avenues, anything other than quietly being right "here".

Stop looking. Be still, right where you are. Take one long conscious breath and see if you can allow life to move you in the next moment without thinking, "I should...", "I need...", "I want...", "I have to...", "I can't...", "It's time...", "I've tried...". Take a look at that "I" and see if you can separate from it...for one conscious breath.

If there is no discernible movement during or after the breath, be with that, and take another deep conscious breath. Again continue to wait for the impulse of life to show you the next move for this form called "I".

Detach from the litany of to-dos and allow yourself, if even for just a few moments, to not know anything. See if you can detect the Creative Impulse that moves through you, gently guiding you, rather than listening to the demands of the illusory self.

You cannot be here and be looking for the self because the self is already here. The challenge is to trust that, exhale, stop believing the mind, and allow life to show you in each moment the effortless magic of Presence.

Seeing and dropping illusion (sometimes over and over), will create an opening just big enough for the light of awareness to be recognized. Once that happens, ho boy, what a good belly laugh you will have.

"We live in a fantasy world, a world of illusion. The great task in life is to find reality." ~ Iris Murdoch

Freedom or Comfort

It is possible to be free in every moment, in every situation, in every emotion that arises. Letting go of an idea that something needs to change for peace to be present is the key to freedom.

Getting comfortable with the uncomfortability of any situation turns down the volume of the experience. Surrender is not a giving up and melting into a puddle of 'it's just no use'. It's simply a relaxing with what has arrived in one's life. In that relaxed state, or stillness, guidance can come through showing the way to resolution, or response.

Reframing the experience from a fresh place rather than the patterned and programmed mind can create a whole new way of being with every experience in every moment. Curiosity can pop the circuits of victim, confusion, and desperation.

Everything that exists is here to assist your growth,

shift, expansion, deepening in some way. What would happen if you faced every moment with this awareness?

What happens when one lets go of the need or idea for whatever is presenting itself to be different?

See if you can notice the programming that has been installed around discomfort. We've been trained to contract, to run from it, to distract, fix, to resist it. Can you consider the possibility that the discomfort you are experiencing is actually You guiding yourself to move in another direction, or to open you in another way?

See how the mind wants to create a story, a great drama about whatever it is that's going on in the moment.

The portal to greater understanding and trust widens when we let go of a need to know what it all means. Tune in without knowing anything and wait for the soft urging of Self to point the way.

As a reminder, ask yourself in the face of every challenge, "Do I want freedom or comfort?" If your answer is freedom, exhale, let go of the reins, and say YES to life.

"We turn to God for help when our foundations are shaking, only to learn that it is God who is shaking them." ~ Charles C. West

Don't Mind the Mind

Where are you? Are you tuned into the inner world while also experiencing the outer world? Are your words and actions in alignment with your thoughts and feelings?

Many are sleepwalking, having very little or no awareness of their bodies or their feelings. They are not here.

We've been trained to project into the future, long for or lament about the past, and multitask right out of the present moment.

While following thoughts, giving them our attention, we jump right out of body-awareness, and are lured into an imaginary world.

A thought is not self-sustained. It needs you for fuel. It needs your attention, your belief.

Don't mind the mind. Don't invest any attention or importance to it. It'll begin to lose its power, and the grip loosens.

Just watch as the thoughts come and go. Thoughts are like the wind, let them blow on by. Let them make their noise like the wind through the trees. You're going to get whipped around if you attempt to follow them. Bring total awareness to the one who is watching the thoughts come and go.

You are bigger than thought.

Bringing attention back into the body is another way to break the thinking-habit.

Ask yourself at any time, "What am I feeling?" Locate something in your body, a tension, an emotion, anything, and go there. Be with it. Sense all of its little nuances. Stay present for all things.

When reaching for food, ask, "What am I feeding?" It's an interesting investigation that tends to uncover unconscious patterns, and in the seeing comes the freeing. Clearing debris from the unconscious can create an opening for discovering the subtle essence that animates all things.

Don't make it a new practice, another doing, a means to an end. Make it the end. Not a doing while hoping for something else to happen as the outcome of a doing, but an inquiry, just bringing more consciousness online. Truly simply being here.

I simply AM!

Are you holding onto something that is more important than freedom? Take a look.

Awaken to the effortlessness of being...the recognition of that which doesn't sleep or wake.

Die to who you think you are. You are the one you are looking for. Reeeeeeally!

"Every thought and every breath is a breath
and a thought occurring in awareness;
and we are that awareness,
that thought-less and breath-less awareness."
~ Mooji

The Chicken Came First

Are you trying to be someone that you are not? You are beautiful just as you are.

Don't let the conditioned world be the benchmark for how you're doing here. It's not yours. Bust out. Follow the prompts of life, it knows the way and your heart understands the language of life. Tune in. Listen. Stop arguing.

The pulse of life is spontaneously arising within you. It no more needs your assistance or direction than the blood in your veins...it's organic, a most natural and perfect process.

There is not something else outside of you that is required for you to be more you. Stop creating more 'yous'...just be the you that you are. You are perfect, and what creates the most change in oneself is relaxing into the one that you presently are.

Life automatically clears out that which isn't true! It'll bring in people and situations to trigger wounds, bring awareness to blind-spots, and it will challenge you in ways you could not image in order to expand awareness and accelerate awakening.

Check in and see if you are allowing yourself to be manipulated by the conditioned world or the programmed mind.

Are you seeking someone else's approval? Are you letting someone's judgment limit the way you move in the world? Relax into yourself, take one deep conscious breath, let go of what you think you know, and allow life to show up as it is organically presenting itself.

Don't look to keep a low-profile, nor a high one. Don't strive for normal. Normal is someone else's idea of how you ought to be. It's not real. Crazy is also someone else's parameters. Just be yourself! You are like the snowflake, free-falling, unique, and beautiful.

How is the wind blowing you? Where is life calling you?

Is there a "yes" in your heart in response to what's before you? If the yes isn't there, then wait for the impulse of life to move you. There is nothing to figure out.

You are the egg and the chicken, however, the chicken came first. You are the physical expression of Consciousness, the infinite source of all life. You are constantly being birthed, discarding the old shell of limitation.

Your truest nature is undepletable, unrechargable, and unmanageable. You cannot control that which is animating you.

It is done, and I am simply the expression of That.

What a relief.

"Instead of constantly thinking, we become still and quiet, and we become conscious of being conscious. This is the realization of I AM, the realization of Being, our essence identity. When we are rooted in that, thinking becomes the servant of awareness, rather than a self- (ego) serving activity. It becomes creative, empowered." ~ Eckhart Tolle

Birthing a New You

There is a dimension within you that is far deeper than the movement of thought. A depth of stillness and a felt sense of connection that is there always. However, if there is a lot of mental noise, you probably won't notice it very often.

Identification with the mind-created sense of self stands in the way of realizing and experiencing the magnificent depths, expansiveness, and freedom of being.

You are more than just a personal history. You are more than the pseudo sense of self. The challenge in discarding the pseudo-self is that those identified with it believe it's who they are.

Thought is like a little cling-on and it wants more attention...so it can grow, so it can feed the mind-created sense of self. Eventually the noise is so pervasive that it drowns out the voice of stillness that naturally comes through you, and is then misidentified as the one in charge. It's possible to allow thoughts to arise without following them or believing them.

Break the cycle.

In the moment you recognize that you have been caught in the magnetism of thought, pause for one conscious breath. Remind yourself, "I am here." Feel your feet on the floor, your bottom on the chair, the cool air on your face, your heart, anything in the realm of feeling to cause pause in the thought-cycle.

Oh the pull, the alluring scent of a thought, as one tantalizing morsel leads to another...

"I think I'll go check the mail...I wonder if that check has come in from the insurance company...it's way overdue...I'm going to call those s.o.b.'s when I get back in and give them a piece of my mind...oh I haven't returned Tom's call yet...better call him first...he's probably mad at me by now...his patience is pretty thin...which reminds me, I need to get back on my diet...I think I'll start that on Mon because I've got that potluck this weekend...darn those vegans...what will I bring?"

Utter clutter, distractions to keep you from being Here. Just here, now. None of it needs thought, consideration, or attention. Presence is all that is ever needed to manage the details of life.

Where is life guiding you right now? One does not need a narration about checking the mail to check the mail. The energy expended in mental dialogue is far more than what would be used in just responding to life's subtle leading.

Oftentimes during the awakening process, the mind becomes even more activated. This may be because it recognizes its demise, it may also be that the intense chatter is part of the process to help short-circuit the mind. At this point in one's evolution, many think they are going crazy. I was convinced that I was losing my mind - and am forever grateful that I finally did!

Hang in there. Drop into body-awareness. Ground. Unplug and be in nature as much as you can. Breathe deeply. Get support from someone who can hold loving space for you, and remind you that you're okay. See if you can be in your process without turning it into a drama, which is just more mental activity.

Dislodging oneself from conditioned, dysfunctional, and addictive thinking can feel painful and scary. Just like childbirth though, the outcome is beautiful.

Let yourself die to the one you *think* you are. You are birthing a new you...the one who is innately free.

"You can be without your psychological mind but your psychological mind cannot be without you. Judge which is the greater and be one with that. Your mind wants a Hollywood freedom, it wants to be a star, but your self is the Universe, stay there." ~ Mooji

One Day at a Time

Who do you think you are? Whoever that one is, is not who you are. As soon as you have an idea of who you are, you've already limited It.

If I'm not all that, what am I?!

Don't look for an answer. It's the sound of one hand clapping. You can't get your mind around it.

Just sit in the space between the thoughts...the stillness. A sense of the truth of your being rises up from the open space of not-knowing.

There is nothing outside of you or inside of you for you to find. You're looking for what you already are.

What's holding it all, even the question? Get under the clutter of mind-activity and touch into the sweet, vastness of nothingness. Be courageous enough to wander in the place of no-control, where the trained mind melts and the heart leads.

Renounce the illusion that the mind can find the truth
if only you let it search just a bit longer, just a bit more
diligently. That is the habit that needs kicking. Stop
going there. When you see that you've picked it up
again, just gently surrender the story, without
judgment, and move awareness back to the heart,
where guidance can show the way.

When I was attempting to get sober, I was told by
many that there was a much better chance of me not
drinking if I stopped going to drinking establishments.
At the time I had no idea what else I might do with
myself, drinking was so much a part of my life, and
what made life doable (I thought).

Suspended in a life I didn't know how to do, the urge
and the cravings to drink were so intense; I didn't think
it possible to not drink. I told myself (over and over),
if it's this bad tomorrow I will drink. Somehow, one

day at a time (over and over), I was able to get sober in 1997.

The habitual pattern of following thoughts, making up stories, seeking answers to questions that the mind itself has created, is just static in the field which gets in the way of realizing the sweet stillness that is watching it all...at peace...lovingly holding everything.

Stop going to the thinking realm, there is another way that is not of the mind. It may seem scary if identification to thinking is strong. Tell your mind you'll come back to it if dis-identification doesn't work for you. Then, one day at a time, just for today, don't follow the mind.

Nothing else is needed to complete you, to make you more worthy, or more spiritual. Nothing else can be more complete, worthy, or spiritual than you. You're It.

The miracle is right where you are.

"Insanity: doing the same thing over and over again expecting different results." ~ Albert Einstein

Just a Guide

Are you in alignment with the natural flow of Life?

What are you feeling? Whatever you're feeling is a signpost to how close or how far your ideas are from alignment with the natural flow of life.

An example:

I awoke with a cold on the morning I was flying to FL by way of three airplanes. From there I was scheduled to fly to Boston to visit with more family, and work. I was uncomfortable, sneezing, eyes and nose flooding, ears rattling, feverish, and one ear hurting. I was told that because I used Miles to book my flight that it couldn't be changed.

Okay. I could have gone into anger, victim, resisting, sympathy-seeking, and complaining about the way things are; that would have been resisting the nature of things. I had a cold. Flow is to move with it. Stay present. Feel the effect of humidity and heat on restricted breathing. Be with every tissue, every ache.

Let out a howl and let some energy move (not on an airplane though). No story needed about how bad the timing is, how it sucks, or how it's ruining my vacation. That would be misalignment with life. That would be resisting the natural flow of life. It's how my vacation was meant be; I only know that because that's how it was.

So, how one is reacting to whatever is present in life is just a guide, or a barometer for how far you've gone into the mental realm believing that it shouldn't be this way.

Pain is pain, feeling it is how the energy can move. Stories about the pain takes one into suffering, and exaggerates the experience. It's fighting with life.

Be still. Go into the body. Take one conscious breath (through the mouth if necessary), and ask life what is needed in the moment, how to respond to whatever the situation is, and then listen.

It may just be saying *rest dear one*.

"Acceptance looks like a passive state, but in reality it brings something entirely new into this world. That peace, a subtle energy vibration, is consciousness." ~ *Eckhart Tolle*

Parallel Realities

Life is vibration, and it is infinite. Everything is vibration humming at different frequencies. If you consciously knew how to shift your frequency, you could do the seeming impossible.

Your frequency is constantly in flux as you move through infinite realities. All potential exists here and now.

The conditioned mind has been trained to see the infinite parallel realities that we are constantly moving in as linear, which serves the purpose of flow and congruency. For most of us, each reality we move into is so similar to the one we experienced in the previous moment that it seems like time is needed to accomplish things, and that it is impossible to reach that which is "gone".

Time is an illusion for the mind to play this game of here, there, and then. It's all HERE and NOW. All potential (and "past") exists in infinite parallel realities.

A fun example...

I've just returned from a one-month excursion on the east coast visiting family, and working. I brought my two favorite pairs of earrings, one on my ears and the other wrapped in a tissue in my wallet. I came down with a Big Cold the day before I left (you may see where this is going). Changing flights at JFK airport on my way to FL, I threw out handfuls of tissues I had stashed everywhere, including in my wallet. It was two days later when the fog lifted from my head that I realized I'd thrown out my earrings.

I had an ache in my heart, as they were a sweet gift from a dear woman, and that's where my energy was focused.

A week later while driving with my mother, my water container leaked and saturated her purse and my wallet. We took everything out so things could dry. A couple of days later my wallet was back in order.

I was in the zipper pocket of my wallet MANY times since the tissue-toss in NY...my license, a credit card, a couple of buss cards, a safety pin, and no earrings.

About a week later as I was working with a client, reminding him of our infinite nature and the infinite parallel realities that are simultaneously existing here and now, it dawned on me that my energy was focused on the loss of my earrings and not on the possible magic of finding them.

Knowing that all potential exists here and now, I then put my awareness (and deep gratitude) to the realm where my earrings were still in my possession, and opened to the possibility of shifting to that parallel reality. I just kept seeing them in my wallet, not needing to know how they got there.

A few days later while reaching into my wallet at a

restaurant, there they were in that zipper pocket, just lying there out in the open.

For the skeptic, these are almost two-inch-long crystal and silver earrings, not to be missed in a wallet pocket with no flaps or folds.

Philip Pullman in The Golden Compass got it when he said, "If a coin comes down heads, that means that the possibility of its coming down tails has collapsed. Until that moment the two possibilities were equal. But on another world, it does come down tails. And when that happens, the two worlds split apart."

This is happening at immeasurable rate with all of reality. Although the "heads" possibility is what's being seen in this world, a frequency shift can show the "tails" world.

Many of us are like the drunken wizard, unconsciously wielding the wand of creation. You are a Creator of incalculable realities. Where is your focus?

Where attention goes is where energy flows, and where energy flows is how life grows.

"How is it possible that a being with such sensitive jewels as the eyes, such enchanted musical instruments as the ears, and such fabulous arabesque of nerves as the brain can experience itself anything less than a god." ~ Alan Watts

Yield

I stand threadbare, shoeless
Peering in the tiny window of a locked door
Thru frosted glass

A flash of squinting light
Heralds a rumble so deep
It shakes the bars around my heart

A chill runs from the cave of my chest
To the top of my head
As I silence the shudders lest they know I am here

Fear sweats in droplets beneath my breasts
Moistening ancient wounds
Lurking in old nooks and crannies

How do I breathe with no lungs
Or speak when words will not come
Tho life continues its undulations

I long for the wind to whisper the answer

For all the quakes of the earth

To shatter what's left of my heart

I yield, not from the presence of mind to do so

And not of someone else's wisdom

But of sheer exhaustion

The door opens and I excitedly push thru

Into another dream

This one of wakefulness

I don't know whether to climb to the roof and roar

Slip silently under the sea

Or weep at Your feet in reverence

About the Author

Shellee Rae, spiritual guide, aka "unTeacher," and healer has been working with people and supporting them since 1998.

Her first book, "Suffering ~ A Path of Awakening: Dissolving the Pain of Incest, Abuse, Addiction and Depression," takes the reader on a 39-year journey through her life, from her childhood years as a victim of sexual abuse, through lengthy addictions to alcohol and drugs, into deep depression, and ultimately to the doors of death. Then a turning point, into 12-step recovery, emotional healing and sobriety, encounters with many spiritual paths, teachers, and methods, and finally to her experience of embodied awakening in 2008.

Since that time she has been guiding people in their own awakening process by gently pointing to the Truth of who they are from the depths of her own realization.

Shellee Rae offers videos, and other material on her website, www.shelleerae.com. You may contact her via the website for more information, to explore a free introductory session, and to invite her to your area to facilitate an event.

Testimonials

"I consider Shellee a true bodhisattva and radiant guide who serves with humility, wisdom and grace. Please consider giving yourself the gift of her deep presence." ~ Joy H., Oregon

Knowing and working with Shellee has been, and continues to be, a true gift. She has facilitated powerful transformational experiences for me that have opened my heart, brought profound insights, given needed guidance, and pointed me in glorious new directions on my evolutionary path. She is infinitely compassionate, insightful, empathetic, loving, and generous, and I am so grateful to be able to say she is one of my most cherished and beloved teachers and friends. ~ Peter B., California

"My Reiki session with Shellee Rae was a truly unforgettable experience. The moment she placed her hands next to my throat chakra I began to feel an intense energy being activated. A feeling of bliss began to slowly intensify until it felt as though I was ready to burst with love and gratitude. A big expansion happened that night and in the days since my session, I have come to realize Shellee's incredibly deep intuition enabled such an exquisite experience to take place…" ~ Steve A., Maine

She helped me release old stuck emotions, let go of old attachments, understand my patterns, and bring deeper peace into my life. She conducts her work in a safe, compassionate, and highly professional manner. I referred my friends to Shellee and they all love working with her. I highly recommend connecting with Shellee. ~ Monika G., California

"...To say I am stunned and grateful beyond belief is an understatement. I consider myself generally to be a "difficult" person to work with. I'm often blocked, skeptical, and have a very tough time accessing deep feelings...I felt my heart open immediately and effortlessly. Enormous chunks of deep, old conditioned patterns were revealed and dropped away

- patterns that had resisted years of work in psychotherapy and other modalities... I'm enjoying new-found space in my life for love, joy and relationship that I didn't know was possible, and I'm hugely excited about the new openings and possibilities that may become available as I continue this work..." ~ Russell G., Oregon

"Thank you so much for the powerful session. . .
Whew . . . it kinda blew my mind.
I'd like to do that again. . .
The spirit that comes through you . . .
It's Peace, It's Love, It's Connection, It's Oneness,
It's Home.
It seems to be the same spirit that comes through me from time to time. But you seem to have much more consistent/good connection/flow.
:) I'd forgotten what home feels like. :)"
~ Bob N., Oregon

"During the time I have been working with Shellee, I have grown to greatly appreciate the nature of her gifts. That being, the presence, patience and love that she has shown me whilst helping me to get that it's alright to be me... I highly recommend spending time with Shellee Rae." ~ Mark R., Australia

"It's funny, but since then [our distant session], I have had more energy, and a stronger urge to do something productive than I've had since the surgery... I'm not sure how this thing works, but you must have done something that was good for me!" ~ Nel M., Florida

Made in the USA
Coppell, TX
22 November 2023